Shadow of a Cloud but No Cloud

PHOENIX POETS

KILLARNEY CLARY

Shadow of a Cloud but No Cloud

THE UNIVERSITY OF CHICAGO PRESS

Chicago & London

KILLARNEY CLARY is the author of three poetry collections: *Who Whispered Near Me*, *By Common Salt*, and *Potential Stranger*, the last also published by the University of Chicago Press. She lives in Aptos, California.

The University of Chicago Press, Chicago 60637
The University of Chicago Press, Ltd., London
© 2014 by The University of Chicago
All rights reserved. Published 2014.
Printed in the United States of America
23 22 21 20 19 18 17 16 15 14   1 2 3 4 5

ISBN-13: 978-0-226-17798-4 (paper)
ISBN-13: 978-0-226-17803-5 (e-book)
DOI: 10.7208/chicago/9780226178035.001.0001

Illustrations on part-opening pages (15, 29, 41, and 51): details from *Untitled* (2004). Watercolor, 14 x 20 in. Courtesy of the author.

Library of Congress Cataloging-in-Publication Data
Clary, Killarney, author.
    Shadow of a cloud but no cloud / Killarney Clary.
        pages cm — (Phoenix poets)
    ISBN 978-0-226-17798-4 (pbk. : alk. paper) —
    ISBN 978-0-226-17803-5 (e-book)
    I. Title. II. Series: Phoenix poets.
    PS3553.L345S53 2014
    811'54—dc23

                                            2014001564

♾ This paper meets the requirements of ANSI/NISO Z39.48-1992 (Permanence of Paper).

for MATTHEW JAMES FLYNN

ACKNOWLEDGMENTS

Grateful acknowledgment is made to the following periodicals and anthologies in which some of these poems first appeared: *American Hybrid, American Poetry Review, Bear Flag Republic, Catamaran, Faultline, Indiana Review, Miramar, OVS, Phren-Z, Poetry Northwest, Sentence, Southern California Review, Xantippe,* and *Zocalo.*

Thank you again, Jim and Gary.

Shadow of a Cloud but No Cloud

Through a panel of controls in the post-Panamax crane cab, the container is raised from the ship and set on a trailer from which it will be transferred, at the intermodal yard, to a train through the Alameda Corridor. Switched through to the Inland Empire and beyond—the clothing, electronics, and toys from Asia are on their way.

From the warehouse in Sparks, Nevada, to fill a catalog order in Emmett, Idaho—a blouse for a woman who will be better when the parcel has arrived. Summer's coming. She slits the tape, unfolds the pale tissue, lifts the thing. Dust on the dresser, powder on her throat, a fine quiet glow on what she has gathered, and a siffle in the blinds, heat leaning on the outside wall of the dim bedroom. The color is different from what she expected. She pulls her shirt off, feels a tingling surge of shortfall behind her eyes.

We watched ravens ransack the truck-stop trashcans, plastic blowing across the blacktop out onto the desert, catching on fence wire, blooms of Styrofoam in the tumbleweed. As long as we were not speaking, I wouldn't hear what I was afraid you'd say. I wouldn't say the words I'd be sorry for. Doesn't the wind need to rest? A motley sparrow turned his working, calico eye to the sun, heated the mites then dusted them. Tending to himself, he looked bad.

There is nothing said to her from which she does not shy. Another word will come, irritate delicate privacy. Seen parts, well formed, finished, don't give. She will not give way. The sores of our voiced care she tends with long rests, rising in the afternoon for a drink of water.

When her mother dares, *You promised to eat*, she is silent. Help is arranged and she goes along with it. Help is a sad song playing in the background. Distance clothes her cooling body, promises to keep her, like dry ice, ever without the middle part.

He pressed his fingertips on the rim of the coffee mug, let up. *I want to know what THIS is.* He swore he wouldn't settle for belief. We ate sandwiches and he went away.

Trucks pass on the highway around the lake. Stuff is transferred at every hour, pottery fired, racked, packed in custom cartons to keep down damage, to eliminate rattle. The enterprise narrows to a delivery at my door. Box opened, the vase rests on its own against my hand.

His question moves up my arm, one cell against the next relaying uneasy wonder. Jet Skis on the lake, summer in the tall yellow grass. THIS is, each tick, the *Good night* we nod as we cross—greeting and goodbye.

The matter resists my touch. The world resists my thinking. Maybe he stopped. Maybe he broke his resolve, gave himself over to involuntary muscles to keep from choking on the stream of marvel.

She taped a note for me on her window, and I one in return; she answered. Now I am expected and will do anything else. If there were another place to look, a periphery, I might bear a thing said and then the waiting. She is four years old, watching my window, and I am counting. If handing over and standing still weren't a trap.

I see through the glass the glare on ornaments. Her Christmas tree was cut to be this exactly, to last as this. Needles dry and drop. We might become friends, set these houses adrift, refuse to promise.

When she stops at the two-thousand-year-old body she is silent. Can she think of her apple in a bag on the bus? We will pass to the next dimly lit exhibit—darkness protects the weave and finish—then to peppy questions about magic, and a wishing well at the end in the light. Here, a vial of berry seeds eaten twenty centuries ago, a leather rag. I look and look away through the north door to a pavilion where butterflies scatter in the April afternoon. I've noted the exits, measured the hour. What I learn catches on what I already know. Her damp fingers trail, lift away from the glass. For her, too, the forms harden.

A four-sided traffic light hangs above the intersection, swaying, dim through the dust. No cars. It changes. Four flat treeless streets reach four horizons. After ten years the woman says, *I never loved you.*

Red train across the Mojave, rose quartz glitter rises in drafts against the mountains, curls back to fall in dunes. Ocotillo whistles for the wind all night. No place. Called waste.

His hand barely against his shirtfront, he leans forward to smell the bitterbrush. Bees. Late sun on the red rock, dark in the deep verticals, engine idling. How can I tell what it is to be alive? Why do we say *love*, or paint pictures of a limestone outcropping? When he climbs back into the truck he leans against me. What is weight? The cab smells like honey.

If we hadn't kissed goodbye a second time, the car coming off the freeway at the Vine Street exit would have hit me.

I am careful when trees move without wind. Careful of what? The dead love me. The evil ones have not secured my signature and must remain attractive. They will not hurt us.

You say the only thing you want now is for me to worry less. You remind me where we sat yesterday, across the ravine, on that ridge. *See?*

As long as the edge of the chair's shadow touches the doorframe, we are alive.

The girl falls in love and wants to be well, is well, and forgets to measure. She is noticed or not in the supermarket by the boy she met at last night's party. The day is bright; she hears thunder, and mist sprinklers come on above the lettuce. Bitterly, the word comes— *Silly*. She is chilled and losing. The list is numbered. Each shape and color announces at once it is against her and at her service. To keep from reeling, she could use her telephone. Her hand is lax on the cool lemon.

Worry touches the loaded brush tip to the wetted paper and the color floods into a sharp-edged shape, darkens to be a thing, my own. Want draws a picture, so the strain is milked.

You smoothed my hair. Your big fingers combed, caught, pulled away so as not to feel the rough spot too long; it was long enough for me to know you had felt it and wonder if you were repulsed. You moved on. I haven't had this thought.

You came into the room where the two of us were talking and you looked only at her. I am not thinking this. I won't say. I will dress in red next time.

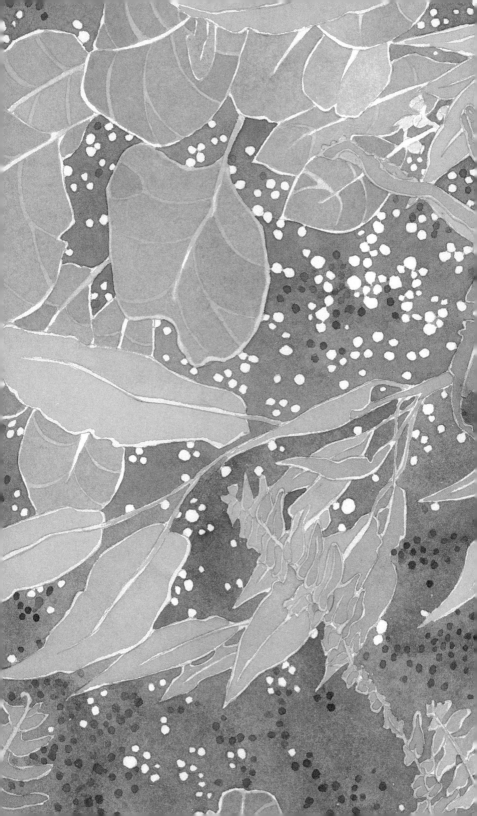

Pigeons nest in the crooks of neon tubes above the man doubled over at the pay phone who presses 9-1-1 for himself while the cop nearby pats down a bored boy. When the ambulance comes, the Metro Rail crowd crosses anyway in front of it, so the paramedics wait.

Hollywood and Western. How thick a medium will we share? Static crackles—a moist breath in contact with heat. *Where'd she get the money?* Wind kicks dust off last year's burn. Ruby glass casts a red shadow. The woman in the wheelchair accepts with a sigh the weight of her caretaker's head on her shoulder.

I say downtown's beautiful at night. But on Saturdays he drives a cab. *What I've seen.* He closes his eyes and fists. I leave him off and head home toward the sparkle, over the four-level stack, this time suspecting that in the dark shafts between the blocks there is a driver whose fare is a perfect fourteen-year-old Guatemalan girl handing him a Beverly Hills address. He can't word the question. She shakes her head, pays him quickly, and drops, glinting, into the deep.

My practice of leaving throbs in the carpet's design. While you talk, shapes spin then settle—bats in a cave. The city whir and repetition of blue accompany the dream of elsewhere. A walkway supports a footfall. Doubt prods the hive.

I watch along the border's stems, count the leaves in case I have to come back. While you tell me what is wrong, again, I trace the figures with my sight in order to finalize: *This is the best road away from hearing what is asked of me.* The single thing forces the hum. Against your *I need you*, a pattern rises in the weave.

The wooden pieces were strung on elastic, which was loosened by a button on the pedestal of the toy. The body collapsed into a pile of colored bits. I eased my push; the doll snapped tall.

The woman stood in front of her husband, her back to him, and she fired the gun, at his instruction, at the cardboard target. He said something else, and she turned, asked, *What?* and shot him dead, by mistake.

And then what?

It can be drawn, she thinks, *if it can be pictured*. It could be any shape, any with error, if she could say, *These are the colors*, if outside weren't called for, song, not called forth, no dreamt dress, invented love, no purpose.

She wanted to be certain of the shapes' edges, before the color bled, to hold the flatness. How crooked his nose appeared in that light. She drew it her own way and was disappointed. Her opinions, once out, were unimportant to her.

The design can be explained. She can rest with it, store within it what the impulse was. They will ask for an account of the painting. She will talk about the shapes.

One woman calls to the other to turn around and come back. *They've found her.* She stands very still to keep phone reception at the edge of the fire road, halfway up Mount Lee. *The paramedics found her in a parking garage. We have to go. Now.* And the other woman says to me, *Look at the horses, how beautiful.* I ask if they need help and she smiles, *No*, and heads toward her friend. Three crows fly above me. One drops a scrap of white tissue paper and another catches it, flies higher and drops it for the third to take. I map their loops in my mind, a pattern in the sky above the city park. The women jog down the road to the gate with their good news. How can it be good news?

I have no say over what my expression does in your head. The trinket was slipped into the pocket, the pocket picked, the cheap treasure lost in the seam of the bus seat. The bus in the ravine off the Ortega Highway is burning. A mole lifts its nose into smoke.

At the crossroads, at the city limits where taxes aren't certain and unusual bargains are struck, I said I was your friend. I wait while you talk. I wonder what you mean. On your shoulder, shade-lace swells. I don't want to hold you still, sun in your eyes, but yes I do. Stay until we are referring to the same, third thing: cat chasing what might be a lizard, might not.

She has put the cup where I can reach it. She's said the cruel thing and gone. Across the grass, ice spills out of a pitcher into plastic tumblers, onto sticky oilcloth in the afternoon swell. At the feeder, a hummingbird drinks and perches, and again. Clear surfaces flash quick spectrums onto the lawn, onto the shadows of leaves.

There is no end to the gifts, no place to put what is left over. To dress the sore, a patch is strong, but close-by the difference makes a weary place. The smart doesn't last. From the glass flower, sugar water.

He rustled in private in the wooden dressing closet next to mine at the pool. Hazy heat reached through the door cracks across my skin to the wet palette floor. The white plastic ball played its hollow double beat on the table in the shade. I never said hello to him. Pale and dark-haired, younger than I, he paddled in the shallow end while near my hold, near my face, water lapped into the overflow gutter. The frozen taffy bar I'd broken melted eye-level on the concrete deck. My mother and aunt whispered. I thought I could save him from the whispered thing.

The game he plays he plays with his weight on one knee, on the press of a few toes. Where to place the black marble, how to look and measure by looking, and have his push work with the measure to put the thing—there—is a way away from time.

Beads of rain heavy on the leaves between his nape and the sky are not included, a late light on the hand he holds behind him for balance is. Narrowed then opened, throbbing slowly like fever's edges, the space is not entirely outside, so his frame wavers, so he was never this, forever this.

What else is now is not now for him. The round glass is shiny between his thumb and middle finger, cool and dead. It will be tossed, will reach, or not, the mark. This matters repeatedly, is broken by hunger, is hunger. He will pitch it to its end, and be free of it.

My feet are soft and quiet against the cool floor. Midmorning I understand there are no birds.

I have gone through the first night, the worst.

Dry gravel ticks, crumbles into rivulets. Sparse grey foliage and its shadow tremble in a dusty wind. I spent half the party saying goodbye.

You hold your T-shirt at the label, pull it up and off your back and lie down.

Why is there still a world for me?

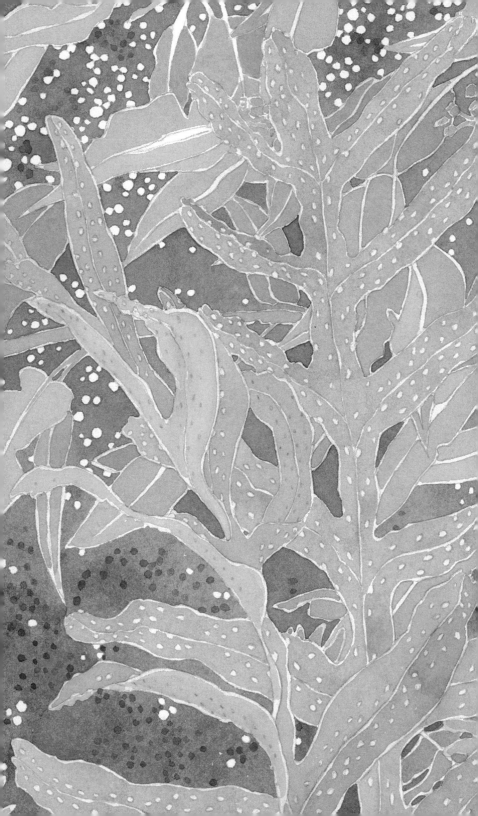

Mama lied, *What you have made is good.* So many gray clay pots were proudly collected at the school gate. *There is no one like you, my darling.*

Thin clouds hold the sharp heat off. Rocked in shallow swells, a drift of minnows pulses. Suspicion hangs in monsoonal moisture. A swirl of pale hair in the bay—pressing forward keeps the weight suspended.

Powdered, loose skin gives, cool against a kiss, receives, *I love you,* which veils with sheer fabric—I love you enough to lie.

At the edge of the Pacific, a speedboat wake taps the shore. The speckle of shadow disperses; castles collapse into their tunnels, and a woman shakes her sunburned boy, *Where's your sister?*

My whispers come back off your skin; we hear our spittle split, our breathing while we hold quiet. They can't hear, can't read what we've written with the dry cleaner's clear wax zipper crayon on the flat blue-gray paint on the closet wall: a phone number, a hideout place—below the elm behind the camellia where the oily soil stays damp, after the last bell when the swing chains hang still. The marks glisten in the angled penlight. *Meet me there.*

Christian's Hut burned down within an hour—dry palm fronds and tikis bright in the August midnight. In the holiday crowd, we flickered and dimmed on the far side of Balboa Boulevard while inside the rented house, Mama watched *Chiller* over her glasses, over her knitting, not not hearing the sirens. Her needles worried the purl stitch. The black-and-white face melting in acid reflected off view windows dulled by salt.

Down to the cold sand to play with phosphorus, we didn't talk about the man assumed drowned, missing two days, his shape, a ruined castle near the tide line. When we crashed through the screen door, laughing for cake, she went up to bed without a kiss.

I sit on the sunny pantry floor and read repeatedly the label on a can of mandarin oranges, its best-by date years past. There will be noise; they will need me.

My hands are exactly as I remember my mother's hands, now gone. The morning itself is gone. Near the stiff hinge and scratching in the wall, I fall through the floors, and when the bottom isn't hit, after a while I start again to sweep up.

Dust rises in dragons, their scales stretching into feathers, into flames, then dust. Tufts of pink insulation whisper behind the plaster: an amen to my anti-prayer. What's been gotten into now?

The beaded velvet jacket Mama gave me is in the attic. The ugly pin Daddy bought for her is locked in my case, the figurine with its various stories, polished and treasured for the version I prefer: clumsy and wild, he brought it across Germany on a bicycle in 1938.

I hand you her silver monkey ring, its belly an opal—another gift she pretended to like. She kept it throughout her forever. The metal is worn thin, the animal's features smoothed, abstract. I'm not sure you will take it.

Electric with the possibility of another demand being jammed onto the list, she says she has to hang up now, and then, *I don't know why I said that.*

There is no split, yet, in the swell of our exchange, but its membrane thins. *Stay a little*, my silence hopes. Hold back for a minute, and stay.

In the story, a poor family lives on bakery fumes, sleeps under the bridge. I try to imagine the smell of bread. I nod at the words when she reads them to me. I am loved, but can't think. Now it's my turn to read. Mama waits. My mouth waters. My eyes water. I bury my face in her dress.

There are always three living under the bridge. I am one of three children. I will breathe against the wall to feel breath against my mouth. I am urged. A chill needles the base of each hair.

I am selected to be *IT* in the Halloween game, blindfolded and spun, handed moist shapeless stuff to guess at. *What do you think this is?* I don't know. All me lost in what I think all of them think. Oh, this is cold noodles, not brains. They know that. I am seen, can't see what they are after.

Mama and I knelt together near the brick edge. She dug holes on the border of the bed, cut flats into squares with a kitchen knife, went inside for the phone. I was by myself, planting pansies in the late afternoon shadow of the house, in the cold, springy dichondra so easily bruised. The plum tree leaves stirred, black-purple, deadly, dark. I wanted her to come back.

I forced open the door. She had fallen against it and was lying on her bad side, which she no longer felt. Now they say it all depends on the extent of insult, and her will. I leave the hospital, trying not to think of the Little Engine That Could. I wanted to give power over to a higher order, but I am yanked back down to the muscle of the visible—will.

A bruise turns from purple to yellow. A broken bottle lies in the sand, danger we might negligently avoid. *Whose arm is this? Mama, it's your own.*

I knew for years I'd be the one to find her. I was ready because I'd practiced. If she had died, would I have assured her, *I am here*? Would I have turned her face from the cabinet and set her head on a bunched-up towel in the hot, damp, and still air, straightened her, pulled her away from the door so the men could enter, out of place in their heavy clothes in the pastel finery and smell of hair spray? Did the rehearsals pay off? Was this a good day?

Over the Sunday crossword puzzle, after the bread pudding I brought her and her usual custard, Mama hiccups. I tell her I can cure her. *Just take my hand and look me in the eyes.* She frowns, says, *Never mind.*

I tease her a little. Her fingers feel cool. She raises her eyes, not long enough for the needed discomfort, then lifts my hand to her kiss, frees herself from me, and reaches for her pencil.

I wanted to lighten his heart. After the cemetery, we could go out to Rosses Point for dinner, walk on the beach. It was difficult for him to untie his shoes; he was uneasy when I knelt to help. Then he started to cry.

We waded quite a ways out in a beautiful place. The beauty was hard to take. We drove north into Donegal. Daddy drank a rum and coke, said he felt better; we'd done what we'd come for. *Every time I picked up that case with her ashes in it, I remembered carrying her on our honeymoon.*

There was no rain the eight days we stayed. He was embarrassed in the hotel that some might have thought we were lovers. When I didn't flirt back with the man at the payphone, the man, to shame me, joked, *Who died?*

In praise of inhibition, mine is the freehand line, traced. I didn't know what would happen; I repeated the wonder at every angle in my mind.

Daddy tapped his foot to Count Basie, took my hand, said, *Relax.* I couldn't plan for the measureless, the sense, in the pitch, of something passing above, how I might flinch and shy. I lied when I said I didn't want to dance.

I can think anything. I pay monthly fees to ward off surprises. The rope, tossed from the bridge to the river, meets its shadow and reflection. What is worried hits the event.

Each rock shifts in Rubio Canyon. Freshly exposed by record-breaking rainfall, the granite rubble is sore pink. I step swiftly as if to settle, pass across.

He's threatening to break out of the facility, my sister tells me over the phone, and then together we say, *It's on the train tracks.* We practice his mind.

Shadow of a cloud but no cloud darkens a tree of night herons. What if there's not enough money for the medicine?

Sky, reflected in the water dish, is a bright, deceptive infinity. The index finger of the empty glove arcs high as if calling for a waiter to clear.

In the hour in-between, expecting the sound of a car, a back door, voices—there should be a way to step through. We did our homework; they had cocktails. We wanted the day to end, wanted it to have been more. Dinner pulled us into dark steadiness. Mama said the only time she felt really happy was when we were all asleep.

Sundown is a bad time for those in care. Routine fails and nameless yearning chokes the works. I am advised to change the topic or the room.

In the yard, the middle values are lost and the bits left shining pull at me. Unease stretches, glimmers in the spray of a clicking sprinkler. Between what's given and what's received I laugh because I can't hold the rare pure thing. An untouched wisteria pod pops in the heat.

Birds clump on the ditch bank that runs along the tracks. While the loud train passes, I can rest for a minute, think of what you might want to hear.

You are chewing, working up to telling me the next troubled bit. I hope that before you swallow, your mind will shift. I could spill my drink. I will. I will awaken the frozen sumac, inspire or torture the cold, slow bee.

This one's going to cost us plenty. Always us. Your money, risk, your anxiety of which I try to relieve you by joking, by putting my index finger to my lips and saying, *Shhh. I think you got away with it.*

In the exit hall, you recognize the old woman by the door. You start to introduce me to Killarney, then, puzzled, you stop. I ask if you remember building me a birdhouse—mahogany with brass hardware. I can't imagine a kind way to tell you who I am.

The dead wear bright slickers and stand beneath the smoke trees. They smell their fingers and remember mice and apples, broccoli plants in the moonlight.

I pull out a weepy cough drop from the back of the bedside table drawer, camphor ice, nametags for his clothes.

If a rat crosses the transom, I should pay the fee and enter the dim garden; what comes to me there will lead me. The gates are closed behind me for the night; I won't have another chance.

A bird's foot curls on air. That lack is a lack forever. There was pure color in the open, a yellow iris in the rain.

I make mistakes alone now that you are dead. In a room, I decide to buy the wrong offering. I sell or hold on. I lose your money.

I try to allow for it, as you would have, but what I find of you in myself is there for others; it won't face me.

When you ordered short on the teak base molding, you placed the gap, not behind the door, but where anyone would notice. You smiled and shook your head. I wish you could see me now.

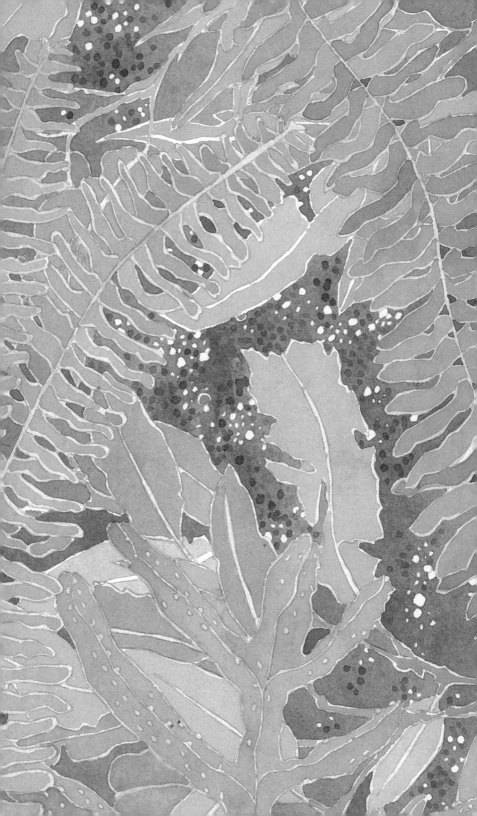

If I pretend to love one I do not love so I won't hurt her, I must love her enough.

To say you will not talk about the boy says a lot.

He and I agreed we'd had good lives, and if we were to die tomorrow we'd have no complaint. Then he died.

One shouldn't say to a friend, *There's nobody I can really talk to anymore.*

The old rain blows down from the trees, and frogs gather in the culvert at the grate. Mice have made their beds of shredded pocket cash. The bird's nest is part cat hair; the feral cat's lair is lined with feathers.

Darkness moves out from between guiding forms and takes on a shape of its own—coyote, deer, fox, the begging ghost, the hungry not-yet-ghost. I look behind me for the hunted. I look forward and the predator has vanished.

There is a pattern, not a story, repetition of shape, change of scale and/or direction, a game of perception: find the hidden hat in the picture; it may be inverted. Shown for only a moment, the tray is taken into another room. How many items on it am I able now to name? This is for the prize.

You heard so well—whispers hurt and silence beat, private in your head. Sharp colors irritated—blue and bottle green.

A strip of haze fastened to the surface of Puget Sound, bleached out Rat Island, and I fed you the clear broth of absence.

Twelve years since you hung up. Handful of beach glass. That I might call you—one shrill red grain.

Gulls on the shore of the lake ran with their mouths open through a low haze of flies, against the background of powdery hoodoos and a pale sky. Dozens of kangaroo rats crossed the highway south of town. Fire flared in the east; white wings flashed in the high beams. Surrounded and entered, I kept moving.

Moorage is still paid on the dead man's boat anchored in the narrow channel; an egret sways on the taffrail through the night. Skimmed off in a tsunami, a lavender plastic flip-flop drifts on the Northern Pacific Gyre. In these five windows, a plume of steam is a chorus of fetches. I try to read them, carry them. I am filled, clean. I am lifted.

A ragged coot fought the current. Pulled under at the pylons, he popped up downstream, was swept away while a man on the radio asked, *Does it make anyone else starve—to sit a minute, midmorning, fully clothed on the edge of an unmade bed?*

I hurry to color in the shape, before I forget why I drew it, before hunger. The tree's reflection bends and flutters on the water wobbling in the wind, in the hollow, which holds still.

We hear leaves stir under the bamboo, the progress of our different pictures—fall wind or possum—and I lie against you. One of us is warmer. One will die first. Two shapes lift over the canyon, their prey hidden or scattering. I smooth your hair. What is this?

There is no approach. Those starts are of another world, unsustainable. I lose the stem of your breath, press these fingertips into that arm and feel both give way. The birds call and call, make an unbroken note.

When we took the lower path toward the observatory, the great horned owl watched still as decision from the sycamore. We stopped together—allowance opening all sides, contents magnified and calmed—to be seen, to be saved from being seen.

In a pause between rains, a spider's filament lifts on rising air, gleams, tests its purchase. Termites swarm, glittering, from the asphalt. Your empty hands lie in your lap on your zippered coat the color of cement. I have treasured up our past; you say it's gone. Our shared dresses, the safety of our fine home—*Lost*, you say. Sunlight waits on the floor inside the new house.

Plastic tarps flap free of their tethers and wave to erosion. If either of us dies midsentence I'll believe in an afterlife. Tell me the start of the story before you go, and I will be with you again.

A smudge of cloud on the horizon, then the pale city halo in the night sky. Quiet on the water—in the bare trees, tinsel rain.

A bright, silent wheel turns on the bayside where the secret flag is raised at midnight. Skiffs push off from docks in the fair harbor.

I don't want to hear, again, *Are you tired?* That's why I bought the boat.

She drops out of order to tie her shoe, kneels to the brick path slick with moss in constant shade. The others—the bare legs of the girls, the boys' gray cuffs—pass nearby, not speaking, on the way back from chapel. River, without a message.

She can see the brilliant dry San Gabriel Mountains. They keep growing, crackle in the heat, shed storms quickly. No one settles there. Whistling through the passes, wind draws out one strand of white hair caught in manzanita. Hesitation.

How long until they miss her? There is not a place for everything. Everything is not in place. The drip on the hose bib fattens but won't fall.

I love waiting here where bees were once kept, in the forest clearing, alone in the cold wishing I weren't alone. I think what I can to make myself ache—how it was when we were all alive and all talking. Mama believed that when she died she'd see her mother; Daddy said he'd be nowhere. I hear their voices in my own, feel their manner in my posture as I bend to pull the Scotch broom while it can still be easily pulled. I am full of them. I tell them so, and that has to be enough. The moon rises, and wood rats rustle in the oak leaves. I watch the light come on in the kitchen, Matt drinking a glass of water at the sink, trying to look through the room's reflection to where I told him I would be.